In Gorgeous Display

In Gorgeous Display

Ugochukwu Damian Okpara

Fordham University Press   New York   2023

Fordham University Press has no responsibility for the persistence or accuracy of URLs for external or third-party Internet websites referred to in this publication and does not guarantee that any content on such websites is, or will remain, accurate or appropriate.

Fordham University Press also publishes its books in a variety of electronic formats. Some content that appears in print may not be available in electronic books.

Visit us online at www.fordhampress.com.

Library of Congress Cataloging-in-Publication Data available online at https://catalog.loc.gov.

Printed in the United States of America

25 24 23   5 4 3 2 1

First edition

On March 7, 2020, in Anambra State, Nigeria,
a queer man was beaten to death by two men,
one of whom lured him through Facebook.
This book is dedicated to his memory.

And to the many others who continue to be victims of
anti-queer violence.

Somewhere there are happy cities,
But they are of no use to me.
—Czesław Miłosz

Contents

In Gorgeous Display

Beautiful Boy with Garlands around His Waist

here / i am not his image / & i envy it / i shut my eyes against what
is left / the crackling softness of life / like communion / desire is a
marathon / a baton waiting for your grip / here / i am not running /
neither is he / i sit with a man for the first time / & we talk about war
/ the government / the shitty country / old times / & every evening
/ i look out for that man / i imagine a son & a father bonding over
dinner / but what is left of life / if not language / memories as pretty
as garlands around the head / i remember his face in a photograph /
his arms open / with me blooming like a flower inside / it is the only
time i remember it open / in another race / i am handing a baton
to god / & his own hands are closed / beautiful boy / with garlands
around his waist / sitting by the fire / back home / only wants to be
seen / like the fireflies around him / i reach for this softness / & begin
to break it like communion / i am making new mouths / all over my
body / & i still fail at one thing / to be held close like a wound onto a
lightbulb / & called kin

What Is Left of Us Is Made Broken and Shy

on the eve of my thirtieth birthday // we returned almost to each other
like the day we first met // it wasn't perfect // but it was close

you asked for my hands // & like a good child // i offered
them to you // you held them so tenderly // like you first held me

our knees grazing the center rug // i got you last christmas
to fill up your home with warmth // you beckoned onto god

because // you didn't know // what else to do with a son's hand
later you'll ask me about god // & i will sit at the edge of your sofa

& recoil into the silence // we are both akin to
you wouldn't draw near // as you would in my childhood days

when you'll rest my head // on your lap as you assure me again
& again // that god made me perfect // & i will think

to myself // how much of my flamboyant gestures
did he make perfect?

In Which I Sit with My Father on a Threshold

i am retracing language as i come undone in my father's arms // i
watch his hands fall apart like a bird's wings // & we haven't killed
anything yet // save the innocence buried within my throat // the
road to exile is nothing but a dim road // & you // in a car with your
hope clinging to the walls // waiting for the light the music harps // i
sit with him // & learn how to thwart the silence inside // i am tired
of running // of falling into every man's hand // in search of a voice to
call me kin // i desire nothing // but for the city to see me in my lush
nakedness // & love me // here // the door opens // & i sit // & merry
out of its hinges

We Are No Longer at the Threshold

it's either we're in, or one of us is out.
father & son, the door shut

against any kind of escape.
we begin again, the archival work.

& yet, i am lost in this history.
this erasure sits on my tongue like a sore,

turning solace into debris yearning
yet again for the wholeness of exile.

i want him to hold me still
with no demand of hiding.

father & son, digging into each other's name
to know how long we've been deserting

our home, only to be left with desire as erratic
as a mob's stick landing on a queer man's body.

he sits across me
& our love eludes

each other, for we are everything
we do not desire. i fold this part

of me akin to hiding,
& lean right into his shadow—

the most that i could get out
of this shared history.

In Which I Sit with My Mother

in the room   i sit with my mother
lately   it is a ritual   we have come to know
                the darkness   humming softly   within my throat
the wounds   caving   deeply
    i am afraid   what's left   of the music
        is cold   & swollen   like a man
running into a noose   only to be left   tender
            i am not particularly   keen   on tenderness
i have known   the gestures   of my bruises
                the room   large   enough   to hold both
broken bodies
we are flawed   & yet   in this version   we are still
    our hands   small & entwined   afraid to know
                    what the future holds
        in my dreams   i am always running to god   always in the
                                                    choir stand
the latin   softly falling   like leaves   out of the priest's
                                                    mouth
            the congregation stunned   waiting for the hymn to
                                            ferry them along
i am sorry   i am unreliable like joy

Portrait of a Boy in Gorgeous Display

& in his garden
we sit side by side
weeding
it is the best thing
we know how to do
the pulling & flinging
of things we find uncertain
like a boy who isn't a boy
he knows
in the beginning
the dream was childlike
& filled with hope
it was easier to name
to say soft & shy
like his mother
but we've moved past this scene
where hope is an egret
we flutter our hands to
& he no longer searches for its end
he watches me lift a weed
in all my gorgeous display
& within he bleeds again
the quiet between us filled
with brokenness
in the years before this
he would slap my hand
the gorgeous display
of a femme boy
& shriek at the loss of a son
but we sit side by side
& we do not speak

We Recognize This Space and All the Promises It Never Held

father's voice
is a familiar wound

he watches me
watch him

press his head
against the mirror

this slithering coldness
he reaches for

to make sense of a son
we are this way

always drifting
like hands parting

at the end of a prayer
we recognize this space

& all the promises
it never held

so tell me about him
this man you love

he says & reaches again
for the mirror

his back turned to me
the quiet ache

that had once known
my small feet & voice saying

if i stamp too hard
daddy promise you'll let me know

i reach for his back once more
the small brown mole

brushes against my cheek
& on its warmth

i watch him weep
into my own hands

Nervous Wound

&   in every room   i am a prayer   striving
                for god's hands
       & although   my throat   is
charred   from years   of running   i still prefer
its safety
                tell me about safety   &
i will tell you how relative   it is
            a boy   keen on survival   runs
from the atlantic   into the nile
i am this way too   & have tasted the ruins
            of many cities
isn't that what queer survival is about   how the idea
                of home   not home
itself   is a nervous wound   then what about home itself
            a boy   runs into his imagination
& cowers   in its safety
       he does not speak   & where there's a doorway
a threshold   a border   his imagination suffices
       he is numb   to the cruelty   of this world

Just in Case I Don't Come Home Tonight

& when i do get to my destination
        & meet a man who offers me nothing
   but a little kiss on my forehead
  gaze onto the universe & let it know how chic our sarcasm is—
our small ritual of safety:
the pictures of men we trade on our phones   before going to meet them
    hold me the way i've held onto
                 the possibilities of not coming back
for we've been nothing but little risks dancing on each other's lips
              & when i do get to my destination
& meet a man who offers me nothing
                  but a split wound

    whose arms i've imagined for so long
      whose feet i'll fall to
but not seek for mercy
            don't fret
for nothing shimmers through the end
          not even this
nor our laughter
   & within the darkness of it   that might erode my bones
      find my small wit
   & place it by the side of the pictures we have
     let that be proof that i've dared to live
a long & perfect life

Logan Theatre

1.
here you lick my sorrows clean & memory eludes my feet
exile can no longer keep them awake
they are wax tablets on which you inscribe *stay*

the night is cold & tragic & still you hold onto me
like i'm the last stick of cigarette not letting go

back home the bloody night would have snitched on us
& men would whisper gay into the night
while our bodies warmed theirs
i swear! i've seen this happen

2.
you kiss me & fear wrings my neck
you can trace this fear to the tremors in my hands

& i swear i can taste death
for grief is the surviving tastebud left on my tongue

my lips on yours mourn our bones & delicate skin

call me paranoid
back home   fear is the language that saves us

Hand

/hand/

depending on
where you stand
a hand
is a failed attempt
at forgetting

To the Manual Parts of My Upper Limbs Distal to My Wrists

i say *manual* & rebellion rocks like a storm in my mother's mouth // she traces history back to the fetus kicking in her belly // even mother knows not the origin // how a body // can be both fear & resistance

i toss my prayers like a bouquet into the night // i'm afraid i might die as the wind // feeble & without a memory to hold onto

but scars are memories our traumas leave behind // & my traumas are alive // pulsing // & bleeding // which is to say // there are no scars on my body // meaning // i flip & flip & flip 'til i arrive at my palmar fascia // where dead boys with songs buried underneath their tongues // live

truth // this is an ode to my fears // they can quake a country // & still have more to go round // generosity got nothing on them

fear gargles in me like coffee in a coffee maker // still there's no pocket to fold the fear away

> meaning
>
> the distal parts of my wrists // hold secrets that are too heavy for my mind // & i learn from this // to unravel answers from them // like the way i see arthritis eat & regurgitate a body into a grave // or old age scaling around them // breaking free from within // or the fear trudging through me

i toss my hopes like bouquets into mother // *dear momma // see me before this elegy fills me up*

I Prefer the Safety of These Hands

i bring them to my face // & kiss // this act
so small // i let it stay // within what is broken
fear clings to my throat // & pulls me
away from my lover // & i imagine
our room being stormed // the loss of time
on our lonely lips // as we make sense of everything
falling apart

If I Die, What Would My Family Write
as My Biography?

1.

i am not buoyant enough to hold joy spilling from a lover's mouth.
also, i eulogize my fears a lot & sometimes i am everything at the
edge of my fingers. my lover holds my hands & whispers *safe* into the
labyrinth of my right ear to calm the tremor dancing in my hands,
but still, this revival crumbles at the foot of my demons.

2.

sometimes the fraenulum underneath my tongue shrinks & fear grips
my larynx until it shuts like a banged door. i want to say *see, this is
where it hurts*, but i say *see*, & break down into tears as though i love
to bask in consolation.

3.

outside my window, the wind blows dust & sand into my
windowpane, & here, i am also a synonym for paralysis. i lie in bed
all day, whirling my fears away. but last night, an effeminate boy was
bullied, the mob turned the street into a runway for him & filled
their bellies with laughter. i sometimes imagine me as him, god
knows, i would bare myself open until death finds me.

4.

if i die, what would my family write as my biography? aside from
educated, maybe. so calm & gentle, cute & cried a lot. he held his
anger tight; even when his face turned red, he still wouldn't let go.

5.

point to a wound & watch me stutter. sometimes amnesia got
nothing on me. i once forgot a razor stuck in my thigh. i once forgot
myself in a chapel, found myself hours later, kneeling with hands
rested on the pew wondering what i was doing there.

6

if my fear succeeds, & maybe you find me in a pool or in the hands
of men burning with rage & bliss, set me on fire & please, gather
my ashes between pages of my favorite book. & in my next world, i
promise, i will come as a happy poem.

Portrait of a Boy with Hands Helpless

where a country   regresses into another
are my hands   soft & helpless

because the night will come   passing
the day will come too   & men who love
men
will run into their dreams   battered

 because home has never been home
        thwart its head   & you'd see men
afraid that their country   will consume them

because a country   can also be a father turning his back at you

Boy Meets Boy & This Isn't about Love

1.

at the bus stop, i am smiling at a man
i do not remember. i hold my hands
to fill in the space of what i have lost.
time's bruise, on my lips like an abandoned
child on a playground. i do not have the
language capable of breaking open
to reveal my deepest wounds;
to plunge me into a stranger's arms in
search of a way out of my memory.
at home, i pick the landline & call my
mother. we do not speak, other than
crying into the phone. mother & son,
borders running into each other, made small.

2.

in my dreams, i am running & scaling fences.
i wake & tremble at the cruelty of memory,
how it forces you to sit still & embrace
what eats into you. i want to reach
for my phone & call my mother, only to be startled
at the audacious nature of memory.
i, a failed attempt at reality, a dream clean of
possibilities, sit by my bedside & cry into the night.

3.

boy meets boy, & this isn't about love,
only the possibility of it. & what is life
if not the fragile breadth of our instincts & fears?
think lagos, think abuja, think orlando, think dallas.

4.

the light pours into my room, & i begin
to look for god. i kneel by my bed, & long
for the weight of exile. the solitude behind
the doorknob is easier to deal with, than a
whole country emptying itself of tenderness.

5.

my tremors aren't self-taught, & for this, i blame
my country & its laws. i want hands chuckled
with laughter & freedom, & not ruins. within
my room, the light fades, & i am sullen with flight.

What I Know about Beauty

i know of the streets   once
          a man lingered
like applause on a walkway   walked me
          into the dark
          to know the depth
of my tongue   now   another
    takes me further   brings me to my knees
       to the point   where language drifts easily
    to god
once a woman stopped   at a doorway
seized the moment with her cloudy eyes
      as i walked past
now   another collapses
     the windows & blinds   have no desire
          in sharing in my terror
but i too   am not interested   in mercy &
its leaky hands
    i kneel on the gravel & feel my bones
shudder
like branches of a tree   being hit
          by the april wind
i   queer
    i   gorgeous
        i   an exhibition
filled with so much   light
      i say to them   *you're not lit until you make it here*

i ask for more eyes   *come behold this beauty*

come dance with fire

                      & see how rage

 begets bliss

you're not lit until you make it here   & yet

     still afford eyes that offer   you the grace

                  of emptiness

Duplex

i linger again in another man's arms,
& yet, this void remains open.

    & yet, the void remains open
    like my country, i carry it on my tongue.

like a country i fail to carry on my tongue,
the wound lingers & eludes language.

    the wound lingers & eludes language
    where two boys fall into the hands of a mob.

where queer boys fall into the hands of a mob,
i lie desperate & empty my desires.

    i am desperate & yet empty of desires,
    for home is a shadow i cannot see.

home is a shadow i cannot see,
i linger again in another man's arms.

Orbit

in that tiny space between our parents' cars,
we moved in circles trying to eclipse each other.

you were a child whose embrace i catered for.
i taught your faithful hands to knot perfect pieces

in my doll's hair, the one mother wasn't willing to buy
because boys like you deserved something mechanical

to play with. & once, i had slipped my hands
into our mother's purse to be able to afford this

secret weaving, we shared.
once, you asked me how a boy behaves

like a girl. i failed to have an answer.

now you sit across from me & i realize
how we are still moving in circles

leaving a space large enough to turn us
into lonely strangers. you fill the space

with more stories of schoolboys beating
into your chest, asking if you weren't man enough.

how your fingers clutched tightly with remorse,
& still, beneath the boys' cruel hands

you did not ask how they intended to make you more dead.

The Face of Memory Glitters with Hope

me, in my lover's hands, reaching for the softness in him. where desire
is bland, i fill in, & let a boy moist pull me to a mirror, & question my
softness. i kneel beside him, & let my hands become one thing. our
fears & dreams crushed within us. the window, far as a horizon where
nothing matters except what lies sober in my hands. we, closing in on
ourselves like the tender palms of our mothers'.   & here in
this city, we are nothing. all we remember is the door back home, a
country whose quiet we've come to know. here, hope is a photograph,
nesting in our mouths. the soft kiss, to the wall that stays.

Notes on Desire

i gulp this sadness like thirst / i want to be cuddled in it / i want to
empty myself in it

———

mother said the first thing she notices about me is my quiet face /
underneath which lies the tremor / so subtle / you'd dream my hands
into a nightingale

———

this absence / this longing / so humble / i strew them like sunlight
into my prayers

———

father wraps himself / up as a gift / says there's no greater education
than this

———

i am never enough / i live in the shadows / somewhere between desire
& envy / i do not wish to hurt a thing

———

at school / i am constantly looking for my image / i see a boy with
coated nails & vaseline as lip gloss / we sit at the love garden to share
our wounds

———

does it hurt where you come from?

———

please promise me this will end

———

last night / i let a boy walk into my throat / i want to please him / i want him to hold me & call me / *pretty* / *my little emptiness* / i want to see the reason to live in his eyes

———

yesterday / he sent / *i dreamt of you* / *which means i've missed you* / *when are we seeing again?* / this longing tethered to me makes me feel more alive

———

clean history is a sham / every day i am running to find a boy who looks like me / let's build a home / where we dream our soft bodies into full beings

———

my parents have two children / both boys / mother wanted a girl / one she could trade clothes with / my classmate says god has a sense of humor / i don't agree / he morphs one into a beautiful helpless flower / that is made ugly by plucking / he finds his humor in the hands plucking it

Host

After Jericho Brown

we want you manly, one we could sit with
at a bar & drink & smoke & flirt with
the wild mouths of girls. sure you smoke?
drink alcohol? what brand? you should try beer,
so no one will know what we do in the dark.
all that femme shit can wait 'til we get to the room.
we don't mind our man being in touch with his feminine side,
it's such a turn on—but not outside.
we want a man, if we did want a girl
we would have gone for one.
when did you start this game? oh! you've not done bannies?
all that dick? all for waste? one day we'd organize one for you.
you need to try it out, man. we want our men to get married.
straight acting! remember, it's a game.
all this game is something we can curtail.
but if you were feminine on the outside,
we would have turned back & bid you farewell.
man up! sure you do not want the receptionist
suspecting we're digging into you?
or perhaps we should walk ahead.
pretend you do not know us, & that you ain't following us.
you're quite fine & calm like a priest.
bad boy! you have nice lips, we must confess.
are you uncomfortable? you should not.
here's a safe space. please, stay awhile
so our brothers can leave. we can't wait to hold you
& hear your soft moans. you moan like a girl?
good! good! you'll make a good partner,
but you might want to start drinking & maybe do weed.

Diary Entry

i tell you this   desire is a lost cause
   its borders vanish like the moon   within the cloud
oh the moon   how lonely & heavy it must be
          i sit by my window
          in hopes the light will find me

—

desbloquear   my phone reads
          this language
devoid of my tongue & hands   is what i cling to
it is my small way   of being inaccessible
       to the world
& its cruelty

—

abracadabra   abracadabra
          i sleep all day   to escape reality & its pity

—

& truly   the world outside   this window isn't mine
so i stay behind these walls   & count
for these hands   empty & charred   are the most honest

—

on the church radio   a song   *count me out of depression* plays
                    the lyrics pull me closer to god
          like fingers   keen to know   the depth of a wound
i kneel by my bed   & pray that god counts me out   of so many
                                        things as well—
malaria   queerness   fever
          poverty   bad eyesight   tremors
fear & anxiety

—

4:24am   note to self:

call the radio   & ask   what we're counting out today

Leaving Sad Things Behind

for c

after you held my hands &   dazzled my face   with a kiss
in search of a song where a broken boy   lives again   & again
i now trade myself for joy   my thighs no longer fit
in the mouth of a poem   they no longer serve as metaphors
for all the things drowning me   i am learning to be gentle
on them   to stay still like freshly dug out grief
& let the night soothe my wounds   i named a burning wound
after you   i do not claim the origin of it   because
the darkness in me   can shield a country & still long for more
last night i woke to find a smile perching on it
i recoiled like a boy knowing fear   with my knees reaching
to comfort my jaw   i called you & you said
one can find joy anywhere
in a room   in a bathing tub   under the rain   behind the door
with my back propped up on it   i imagine you saying
see joy lies everywhere
i tried swimming again & god   there are so many metaphors
in the pool about dying & holding peace like a marble
i love how the water soothes my body   even though a friend
let me float on his hands   later he'd say something about having
drowned in my twitter bio & how he was afraid to lose me
i changed my twitter bio to   poet   writer   & everything colorful
see how i tilt toward light   *do you notice*
i also stopped reading sad poems like you suggested
fuck i've been so blind to birds & cats
do you know how many happy poems they hold
a cat is in my trashcan   ransacking for food
i do not move from my spot   i imagine you saying
see joy lies everywhere even a cat knows that
i'm learning to leave sad things behind like poems

about gender dysphoria   & me
i held my phone today   to take a mirror selfie
god   there's so much heaven in my smile   *can you see*
it melted like ice when i saw the picture was blurry
i wish you were there to witness my tremor
i held my hands afterward   to calm the tremor
i did not curse or hate myself   unlike before
i read the love poems you wrote me about us revisiting the moments
in a large hotel room   that made our bodies cramp into each other
where you asked if i was suicidal
& i felt seen for the very first time
then you held my hands
& dazzled my face with a kiss
in search of a song where a broken boy lives again & again & again

What Escape These Hands Can Tell

& again   the light falls   back to the walls

      & i envy it   & forget   what memory   chooses to cradle

     & what it chooses   to fade   still   i've known these hands

                                             too well

                       & what escape   they're

                                 capable of telling

what wounds   they hide

here   i sit with the night   & watch

             i am always watching   what leaves

soft   like language   a mother's arms holding the remains

    of her child's body   who left on his terms

now   the queerness   all gone   she holds the stillness

& dreams of ways   to love it   harder   back to life

their hands   twirled into each other   a failed attempt

                                        at holding

& what hides   within   their gentle fists

     comes undone like a leaf   swirling in autumn wind

That Night

the night you witnessed my tears & i on the kitchen floor,
you poked my ribs to understand why a child nurtures grief
in the mother's palms. i do not tell you that i am fading away
from home, from everything that is meant to pull me close.
i do not say how my body is a cliché. nothing new, just old
scars revisiting memories, that night is a route to a journey
long started. & it's exhausting keeping histories on thighs,
mapping death & waiting on it.

Self-Portrait as White Spaces

        amnesia fails me yet again   & memory   rocks me   like a
toddler in its arms   with nails dug deep   into my skin
           everything i hold onto   ruins me   my feet
have grown weary   whacked   from running
joy crumbles   like paper   each time i mold it   to call it a
minaret here   like a child   solitude sits on my shoulders
& recites litanies of broken men   who left home to mend

i will come home & i will loan you my sinews   then
i will leave
        to know how far   i've eclipsed exile   but   i won't
leave you empty   i will leave you   with the last memory   of me
as braille &   you as hands   reading it

both darkness   & light are channeled   into   our bodies
like   intravenous infusions   but   there is no light here any
longer   we've used mine   to reawaken   yours
& now you spend your time   in search of   a speck
of reflection   in me but we bring ruins   like
        souvenirs to ourselves   until every minute of us   inherits
them   & still
        we perform autopsies   on the wrong bodies

In the History of Belonging

please   trace the perimeters of my body & let me know
if this desperation for a place to call home would gag on it
also show me where the chrysanthemums sprout in my wounds
rejection is the language furrowed in my mother's tongue
& in this history of belonging i lie in a stranger's arm
all bloodied   all homo   all femme   in search of home
it goes razz   smooth   melodious   all the things i cannot hold
& then it fades leaving no glimpse for me to catch
i pick myself up   then my clothes   then my desperation
all with a heavy stench of sweat   cream   & cum & cum
in the cab i wonder if the passengers see the filth in me
the primordial loss within itself

All My Friends Are Terrible Photographers

& i too, have been quiet about this.
i hold the door to our lives

light as a prayer & watch.
each of us, barely leaning

into our lovers' arms—
this hiding we are so keen

on breaking will likely
be the end of us.

in the bar, we are boys seizing
the moments with our rowdy laughter;

within us, we are lovers longing
to hold the true face of memory—

even as minute as stillness.
but the pictures we have of this evening

are all blurry, a testament
to our failed attempts at being.

At a Queer Safe Space in Lagos

here, we are clean of home & its hunger.
we lean into each other's arms & this
is the only time we are free & wild.

we are fourteen, in a closed space
untouched by the moonlight drifting
past us. the only thing that knows us too

well is the doorway, where our masks
like doormats lie heavy with our pasts
& the future we might return to. but still,

we sit past our curfew, the sour taste
of desire lonely on our lips, & still
we laugh—truly, & imagine a city

filled with laughter & embrace,
another, whose tongue cannot tell
the weight of exile. the boy beside me

pukes as though ready to take his shell
& crawl clean, right into it.
we'll always be dreamers, he says

in muffled tone as he cries into my arms.
i hold him tight, the way i am taught
to be hopeful, & respond:

but the beauty is in how much escape we can hold.

The Emptiness Born Out of Escape

i sit by my window & watch
the vastness of what lies beyond,

the nest too, by my window, knows this—
i wonder what song the emptiness

born out of escape chimes?
i grip my windowpane.

it is the only thing i trust to hold me still.
not the boy who assured me of safety,

not the other boy full of metaphors,
who called me a dog & asked that i be chained.

i am wary of these hands akin to rust.
of these legs capable of walking into ruins.

i sit with my sister
& fail at my attempt at cracking a joke—

even though much of queer survival
is based on masking.

in my room, i listen & dance to my favorite playlist,
even the silence afterwards could not halt this lonely dance.

i close my eyes gently as a prayer
& ask god for one thing— an end to this reality.

though life trembles in my hands
begging for more embrace.

i sit again & watch,
a bird peck at ants.

here, everything eludes language,
but how much of this city can hold me again?

i've lost the urgency to count,
but i remember how lonely i was in their midst.

in the abandoned building i dreamt of flight,
of the boys before me who have come & gone,

who also saw last, the unpainted walls
that reeked of violence, & of death,

& of betrayal, & of the promise that brought us here.
how close we were to burning,

how relishing the road afterwards deemed.
within those walls, i have known desire,

i have known how hope eludes a queer body—
the movement swift like waves.

Biafra War Song

here
      i see a man
folded lightly   into the residue of a war
he sings: *i will loyally give my gun to someone else to fight for fatherland*
                    biafra take my boots off when i die
a song whose emptiness
                    i've always known
        a song that even history cannot remember
his feet   slightly apart   & agile with terror
he reminds me of my mother saying: *what is rooted will always*
                                lead you home
while holding my wrist   in one hand
        & my passport in another
our shared tears
    the only thing left
    between a mother & a son
      but something in the way   he finds hope in defeat
          makes me want
     to reach into his arms & have those lips
once   starved & battered   yet attuned to hope
what more can i long for
               but bear with me
                 for this is all I know—
         the escape
                dims
                  with reproach

Ars Exsilii

we were young & had mad mouths
we wanted to be ruthless
we hid behind the garage
& took turns tasting ourselves
'til we became nothing but boys
empty of desires

we knelt beside our fathers
& asked to be forgiven
we were called taboos
a menace to the society
we watched our fathers & brothers
pull their belts & everything
we knew of them fell apart

the songbirds believed they were chic
(at least that's what matters)
they wouldn't shut up for a second
they had mad mouths 'til the depth
of their tremors became a currency
for freedom

during the holidays we played games
held a handful of sand
to tell how much escape it knows

we became dreamers
we became sands
poured into hands
our homes
the spaces between our fingers

in a faraway city
we dreamt our faces
into lonely guitars
a stranger's fingers
soft
harped music out of them

we trembled at the sight of our fathers
we were called failures & our love
blamed for our relapse at school

at school we were asked which of us
was the man & which was the woman
& then we were asked to catwalk
so they could make the choice

we learnt about safe spaces
& ran right into them
we closed the windows
& began to see the light
within us
we were enough & yet clumsy
to touch

now the window is our favorite thing
we pull ourselves to it & cry
we miss our mothers & sisters
we break the window
because we envy how much
it can take in without shying away

Peace Lilies

maybe the peace lilies are all i've got.
i tend to them the way i care for my losses—
to be present & always with hands afraid
of ownership. i cannot shake this off.
i offer my presence & that is enough.
my creator, perhaps, might think of me
as a competitor, but then again, i have
no desire for that. i sit with the peace lilies
& i am well aware of how it must be
to live a life where you are always waiting—
the glitters of life like kites hovering
in the cloud with a promise of descent.

At the Airport Terminal

we hang around each other
holding hands
afraid to close
the tiny doors of our lives

like my milk teeth then—
despite hurting so much
had space under my pillow

how close i desired
to hold the promise
of the empty spaces

we're drifting past each other
walking to new destinations

i imagine you leaving my room
as messy as i had left it—
just to preserve my presence
the promise of the empty space

at the departure hall
my flight is announced
& suddenly exile is a swollen wound

that i desire no pleasures
in tending

Joy for Yet Another Night

tragedy hovers over home // with my name stuck between its fingers // i scream to reach salvation // but my voice echoes over the grave // chaperoned by my people // forgive me // my story seems faux like moonlight tales

> *isn't home meant to bring us close*
> *to sing lullabies to soothe our racing hearts*
> *kiss our ugly pains to sleep*

there's a lineage of men running // to lick their griefs clean like the moon // i've traced survival to their arched feet // their toes are fragile from eulogizing forgotten memories // in their presence // joy falls like freshwater // & we unfold & fold into our bodies // more buoyant to hold joy for yet another night

Exile Leaves You at the Foot of Desire

We who are endangered will keep
searching for a place to call home.
—Romeo Oriogun

here, loneliness cowers in your bones & shudders your body into a broken elegy. exile leaves you at the foot of desire begging to know joy again but desire sometimes makes no room for the permutation of joy. here, at night, your father's ghost hovers over you, digs its fingers into the core of your dreams to harvest the reflections of joy. your mother calls & calls & calls & you do not answer. she calls & calls & calls until tremors frolic her fingers & she counts you into her losses again—the first time was when you could not contain your hunger in the cinema & you kissed the boy & felt it was right. you did it again, this time with hugs & tears & although it was dark, still lynching found you & left the both of you at the mercies of life. your mother's call comes again & your ringtone becomes the voice of home humming behind you to come witness joy *but it's all a façade, it's all a façade, all a façade,* you whisper to yourself to drown the voice.

A Ritual about Home We've Come to Know

at a bar in memphis, i sit with a man,
& we talk & trace the rims of our drinks.

it is the closest we've come to understanding exile—
that endless loop of desire & loss.

we ask each other where we come from
& then, insist we're worth the warmth of home—

this lonely assertion, breaking a dream
into reality. he asks what i miss about home,

& i tell him its failure not to hold me
without a mask. i ask him as well,

& he says he longs for the voice of his childhood.
i watch him key in his mother's number

into my phone, & i think how cruel it is
that memory is all that we've got.

we watch the number dial, a voice
rattling out *hello, hello, hello* . . .

like a hymn. & he keeps mute,
only, sobbing into my hands.

Survival

in the club, you danced like fire, spilled your grief like gin, while i, in
a room, knotted my body into all rigid things to becloud my thirst for
men.

•

*fear knows how best to sit in a room, knows how to shrink until it ripples
into your body.*

•

you danced & flickered like candlelight, tried so hard not to lean into
a boy's arms & mourn all the things eating queer boys up.

•

you tried hard, because you could be another chijioke, whose bones
now serve as maps to dead queer boys whose last prayers were ashes
falling on burning tongues. or another ifediuto, gulped whole by
disease, whose bones outlived his flesh on his dying bed, devoid of the
smell of antiseptics. *how could he tell where drowning began?* or me,
who misread a blackmailer's lips for a lover's.

•

see, i am still shrinking while my nudes spread like pox on my
facebook timeline.

•

you did not cuddle my sadness with me.

•

instead, you left to live in a club, because each time we see the
morning sun sneak into our rooms like riflers, we bless the universe,
for we now are a miracle.

•

but there you were dancing like it was your last night.

•

still, i know you were yearning to live, the way your eyes failed to gaze at the waist of boys twisting into a hunger you wanted to fill with your mouth.

I Practice to Get Hold of Myself

to carry // my body like a child // away from ruins // but paranoia
chews me up // 'til it regurgitates me // into the chrysalis of wreckage
// where i sometimes trace // the genealogy of pain // sometimes
a poem is a truth // a witness // that we've tried to hold onto life //
even though it scalds our hands // as hot tea onto a tongue // i want
to melt away // into the cold hands of oblivion // to tremble at the
sight of light // behind my throat // where father is a gardener // are
all the things // that i cannot name // my therapist must think of me
as a sulking child // he dips his hand / into the core of my throat // in
search of answers // you know // sometimes healing can be invasive //
to see // how much you've stomached

tonight // i cling to smaller things // like tears // & tonight // is also a
witness // that i survived

I Have Been Thinking about Worship

After Donika Kelly

since i lost my name in the fields
i go back in time to the cathedral

where at fourteen i first learnt
my desires to be ashes submerged

in water— a failed attempt at resurrection
i kneel at the front pew

because i want to be this close
to god when i seek for a mouth

//
oh lord
i ask that i be saved

not battered

i have no desire
to avenge what's gone

//
dear lord
how long have i been gone

& how long
have i been hunted

//
once a boy in my class wrote
adam & eve not steve in my text

years later another with a bamboo
will place it across a field

he will ask that i pass under it—
a crossing

baptism of a new faith
as i in turn shelter more wounds

he would hold my hands
& bid me farewell

ask to see me again
for updates about my queerness

//
dear lord

what i know of eden
i know against my will

Prodigal Son

& again i return to god
in search of a way into ease

i shut the doors & windows
to signal an end to this race

i ask him to see me & perhaps
leave me clean of the hunger for home

i will his holy hands to hold me
in the dark where need be not

of language & exile & a country
turning its back on me

A Ruined Candle Wax Still Breathes Itself into Shape

i've lost count of the queer bodies burnt on this way
i've also lost count on how many queer bodies
it will take river niger
to quench the thirst of onitsha men & women

like water   we take shape
douse our light
& we will brew colors
for our bodies hold a spectrum

ozomena   my lover
says *nothing would happen here*
let's puff our pride like cigarettes
& then wear it like a halo

we hold hands
& tremor becomes the impulse
trudging through our bodies

although   we are in south africa
but a bird remembers its way home
what happens when the owner destroys its nest

i want to hold onto him
like a figurine holding onto dust in kaduna
inhaling the harmattan air

i know   a rainbow is an anagram
for any color it wants to be
we will make nigeria out of it

in my dreams
my feet no longer spell fear
nor jail
nor death
everyday i wake to *ozomena*
moulding nigeria into shapes of tolerance
he is hopeful like a mother
awaiting her only son after a war

Acknowledgments

I would like to express my immense gratitude to the editors of these publications where some of these poems were first published: Sundress Publications, *Ruminate Magazine*, *Fourteen Poems*, *20.35 Africa*, *POETRY*, *The Penn Review*, *Poetry Wales*, and *Salamander*.

As always, to the SprinNG fellowship and the University of Mississippi MFA Creative Writing Program for their interest in my work and the continuous guidance from my professors, mentors, and peers.

Also, to the team at Fordham University Press for seeing my work and tending to it with care and attention.

About the Author

Ugochukwu Damian Okpara is a Nigerian writer and poet. He is an alumnus of the SprinNG Fellowship and Chimamanda Adichie's Purple Hibiscus Trust Creative Writing Workshop. His works appear or are forthcoming in *Poetry Magazine*, *Poetry Wales*, *The Masters Review*, *Lolwe*, *The Republic, 14 Poems*, *Ruminate*, *The Penn Review*, *Salamander*, and elsewhere. He is the author of the poetry chapbook, *I Know the Origin of My Tremor* (Sundress Publications, 2021).